The Best Of *The Mailbox*®
Bulletin Boards
Intermediate Edition

Our favorite bulletin boards from the
issues of the Intermediate edition of *The Mailbox*® magazine

Editor In Chief:
Margaret Michel

Editors:
Becky Andrews
Irving Crump

Artists:
Marilyn Barr
Jennifer Tipton Bennett
Cathy Spangler Bruce
Pam Crane
Teresa Davidson
Theresa Fogelman
Susan Hodnett
Sheila Krill
Becky Saunders
Donna Teal
Irene Wareham

Cover Design:
Jim Counts

Copy Editor:
Laurel Robinson

Typographer:
Lynette Maxwell

About This Book

The Best Of The Mailbox Bulletin Boards Intermediate is a collection of the best bulletin boards published in the Intermediate editions of *The Mailbox*® from 1988 to 1994. It was designed to provide an extensive collection of motivating, teacher-created, easy-to-make bulletin boards for today's busy teacher. All of the displays involve student participation and make attractive classroom displays.

The book is divided into four sections: Fall, Winter, Spring, and Anytime. There are 90 illustrations of bulletin boards which include complete instructions as well as reproducible patterns.

©1996 by **THE EDUCATION CENTER, INC.**
All rights reserved except as here noted.
ISBN# 1-56234-148-0

Manufactured in the United States
10 9 8 7 6 5 4 3 2 1

Table Of Contents

Fall

Fall Bulletin Boards ....

Greet students this year with an eye-catching bulletin board focusing on character development. Enlarge, color, and cut out the lion pattern on page 54. For extra appeal, cut the word "ROAR" out of two colors of construction paper and mount as shown.

Mary K. Good, Seaford Christian Academy, Seaford, DE

Help students hit the road to success with this motivational board. Cover a bulletin board or wall space with old high-way maps. Cut dark-colored paper for the road. Make five or six copies of the road sign pattern on page 55. Brainstorm with students several rules of *your* road—rules that will help make the year a successful one. Choose the top five or six suggestions and have students write them on the signs. Next duplicate the auto pattern on page 55 for each student. Have students write their names on the autos and add any details that they desire. Post the signs and autos on the board as shown.

Sandra McKee—Gr. 4, Skyview Academy, Memphis, TN

Keep your herd in a helping "moooood" all year long with this easy-to-make display! Duplicate a class supply of the cow pattern on page 56; then write a student's name on each one. Duplicate the bucket pattern (page 56) for each classroom job. Attach the buckets to the bulletin board with a cow beside each one. Keep the extra cows corralled at the bottom of the display. At the end of each week, head 'em up and move 'em out to different jobs!

Karyl Kimmel Molchan—Gr. 4, Churchill Elementary School, Homewood, IL

Greet parents on Open House night with a display of class pride! Have each child draw, color, and cut out a self-portrait. Mount each cut-out drawing on construction paper and label it with the student's name. To give the display an eye-catching dimension, enlarge and color the Earth pattern on page 92 to add to the board.

Jill Shoffner—Gr. 4, Fernbank Elementary, Atlanta, GA

I'm A "Pizza" The Fourth Grade!

No matter how you slice it, this student-created bulletin board will be a hit! First enlarge and color the chef pattern on page 57. Next provide each student with a wedge-shaped sheet of art paper. Instruct each student to write his name on the wedge in large black letters, then add small symbols on the wedge as pizza ingredients. These symbols should represent interests of the student: hobbies, sports, favorite books, etc. After outlining the ingredients with a black marker, have each student color his pizza slice bright red.

Perry Stio—Gr. 4, M. L. King School, Piscataway, NJ

Start off the year on a positive note! Post a supply of blank reward notes on a small bulletin board. When a student observes a classmate being kind, courteous, or helpful, he can congratulate and recognize her by filling out one of the posted notes. Students will jump at the chance to "write each other up"!

Joanne S. Curran
Old Bonhomme School
Olivette, MO

STEPPING INTO FIFTH GRADE

There's a lot of stepping action on this back-to-school bulletin board! Mount the title; then have students draw detailed pictures of their shoes to complete the display. Extend the activity by challenging students to find the lengths, widths, and areas of their shoes.

Ruby Pesek—Gr. 5, Elisabet Ney Elementary, Lake Jackson, TX

At the beginning of the year, have each student cut out a large circle from bulletin-board paper and divide it into sections. In each section, the student writes a clue about himself. Collect each circle and place it in a large, manila envelope labeled with the child's name. Post a new circle each Monday. On Friday, unveil the student's name by asking review questions. Each time a student answers correctly, he may guess a letter in the mystery student's name. Write the correct letters on a laminated "letter board" as shown. After the mystery student's name is guessed, just wipe the letter board clean and it's ready for the next week's mystery!

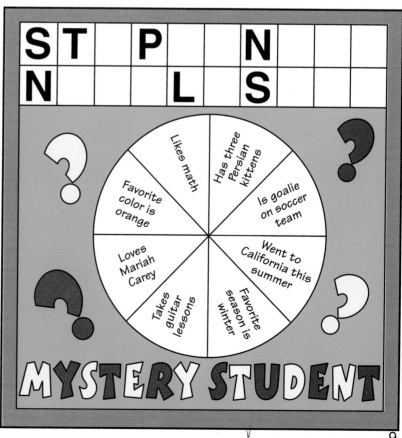

Start the new year on a positive note with this student-made bulletin board. On the first day of school, have students brainstorm words and phrases that can be used to praise someone. List answers on the board; then assign one to each student. Give each child a 5" x 7" piece of paper to decorate with his word. The result—a colorful display packed with encouraging words to share with one another!

Bobbie Harris—Gr. 4
Oñate Elementary School
Albuquerque, NM

Motivate your students to read, read, read with a colorful, anytime display. Enlarge and color the worm character on page 59. Duplicate a class supply of the apple pattern on page 58 on red and light green construction paper. Have each student write her name on a pattern. Attach all of the patterns around the worm character by stapling each one near its top. For each book that a student reads, punch a hole in her apple. Reward those students who read a predetermined number of books.

Connie Halder—Gr. 4, Christ The King School, Mt. Carmel, IA

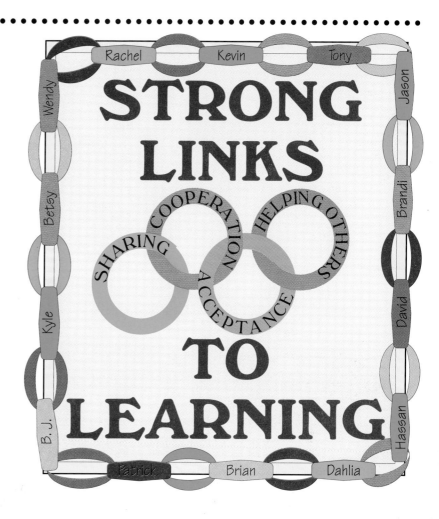

If you need an easy display for Open House or a quick back-to-school motivator, this is it! Talk with students about the qualities necessary for a positive classroom; then write their responses on large, cut-out links. Cut a slit in each link; then join them together on a bulletin board as shown. Have each student decorate several strips of construction paper with his name. Join the name links together to make a colorful border.

Jan Drehmel—Gr. 4
Chippewa Falls, WI

Collecting compliments is a year-round project for your students! Compliments given by other staff members and adults are recorded on cutouts and displayed on our classroom compliment tree. The students are rewarded after a predetermined number of compliments are collected. To increase the longevity of the bulletin board, laminate the tree and cutouts (patterns on pages 60 and 61); then use a wipe-off marker for programming. For variety, different seasonal cutouts (such as apples, flowers, and snowflakes) may be used each month.

Chris Christensen
Marion B. Earl Elementary School
Las Vegas, NV

Use this snappy display and the accompanying "credit card receipt" on page 62 to encourage good homework habits. First draw a giant replica of an American Express® credit card as shown, personalizing it with your name and a desired time period. Next duplicate a class supply of the receipt pattern (page 62) on colorful paper and attach each one to the board. Affix a sticky dot or a small sticker to a student's receipt for each day that he satisfactorily completes his homework. Reward students when they have earned a predetermined number of stickers.

Gena Capps, Dalewood Elementary, Nashville, TN

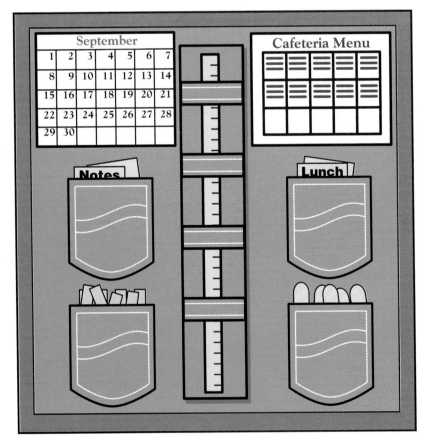

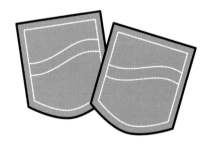

Turn an old pair of jeans into an eye-catching organizer! Cut a piece of denim fabric to fit a small bulletin board. Cut the waistband off an old pair of jeans; then sew it onto the fabric to make a yardstick holder. Sew pockets cut from old jeans to the fabric to hold attendance slips, Band-Aid® bandages, and other important items. Add a calendar, a lunch menu, and daily bulletins to the display. Now everything is right at your fingertips!

Barb Witteman—Gr. 6
Jim Hill Junior High
Minot, ND

"Boo-tify" a hallway bulletin board while advertising intriguing mystery books your students have read. In October, have each child read a mystery book. After completing a book report, have each student label a paper tombstone with the book's title and author. Finish the spooky scene by having students add ghostly visitors and tissue-paper flowers to the ghoulish gravesites. Use the patterns on page 63 if desired.

Marilyn Davison—Grs. 5–6, River Oaks Elementary, Monroe, LA

Encourage good behavior with this seasonal board. Label leaf shapes (patterns on page 64) with vocabulary words pertaining to good behavior, and attach them to the tree (pattern on page 61). Pick a leaf daily and discuss the word. Place the leaf in the basket when finished. Have each student write a sentence describing how he demonstrated that word during the day.

Tonya Byrd
Sumter, SC

13

Create an appealing display that's perfect for showing off fall's finest student work. Staple a large orange garbage bag (the type decorated with a jack-o'-lantern's face) to the board, leaving the top unstapled. Stuff wadded-up pieces of newspaper between the board and the bag to make a three-dimensional pumpkin. Tie off the top of the bag with black ribbon. Duplicate a leaf pattern on page 64 on red, orange, and yellow construction paper. Have each student select a piece of work to display; then have him write his reasons for selecting the piece on a duplicated leaf. Staple each child's leaf and paper around the pumpkin. The Great Pumpkin never looked better!

Gena Capps, Dalewood Elementary, Nashville, TN

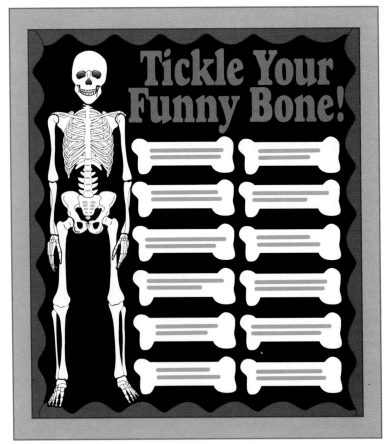

Ghostly giggles will fill the room when you and your students make this seasonal display. Pin an inexpensive skeleton cutout on a bulletin board. Duplicate a supply of white paper bones (at least two per student, from the pattern on page 105) and stock your reading center with plenty of riddle books. Have each student label one bone with a riddle and another with its answer. Instruct the child to tape his bones together at the top, placing the riddle bone atop the answer bone. Pin the bones on the board. Start each day in October with a riddle from the board. Oooo, that tickles!

Suzanne Hammer—Gr. 5
Louisa-Muscatine Elementary
Letts, IA

Here's a bulletin board sure to scare your students straight to their dictionaries and thesauruses! Write one Halloween word on each construction-paper tombstone (see the tombstone and the ghost patterns on page 63). Have students write synonyms on the tombstones. Students can also use the words in Halloween stories, songs, even raps!

Mary Chmelar—Chapter 1 Reading Teacher, Keota Community Schools, Keota, IA

To create these pumpkin personalities, each child cuts out a pumpkin shape from a large sheet of orange construction paper. He mounts his pumpkin on a black sheet of paper; then he cuts out facial features from old magazines and newspapers and glues them onto his pumpkin. Use the pumpkins for creative-writing starters or display them just for fun.

Diane E. Whiton—Gr. 6, Mechanicsburg Area Intermediate School, Mechanicsburg, PA

The Thesaurus:
Where Words Of A Feather Flock Together!

Colorful word birds flock to this seasonal display! Duplicate the patterns on page 65. Have each child write a tired word such as *said* or *get* on the turkey; then have him use a thesaurus and a black marker to label his bird's feathers with synonyms. For a 3-D effect, accordion-fold a small strip of paper. Glue one end of the strip to the turkey and the other end to the feathers before attaching the bird to the board.

Deborah Marik and Ruth Lees—Gr. 5, Southeast Middle School, Ravenna, OH

Celebrate Thanksgiving with this simple, yet timely, door or bulletin-board message. Enlarge and color the turkey pattern on page 66. If desired, have each student add a colorful index card labeled with things for which he is thankful.

Linda Maxwell, Edgewood School, Homewood, AL

An "A+" Thanksgiving

+ Your Blessings
− Your Troubles
× Your Deeds
÷ Your Kindness

To make a good work display for all seasons, duplicate the owl pattern on page 67 for each child. After students color, cut out, and label the owls with their names, mount the birds on a paper tree. Have students use the patterns on page 64 to make fall leaves for the scene. In the winter, remove the leaves and add student-made snowflakes. For spring, have students add green leaves and tissue-paper blossoms.

Courtney Lemmons—Gr. 5, Pioneer Intermediate School, Noble, OK

Display this colorful gobbler and watch your students' vocabularies grow! Enlarge and color the turkey head pattern on page 68. Cut a slit where indicated and insert a paper clip before mounting on the board. Have each student trace and cut out a feather from a large piece of construction paper. The child labels his feather with a new vocabulary word. Have each child introduce his word to the class before stapling his feather to the board. To turn the display into a ready-to-use learning center, clip a task card to the turkey.

Sample task cards:
- Use five words in a story about getting lost on a turkey farm the day before Thanksgiving.
- Write the words in alphabetical order.
- Give the parts of speech of ten of the words.
- Use five of the words in sentences that show their meanings.
- Study the spellings and meanings of five of the words. Have a friend give you a quiz on the words at the end of the week.

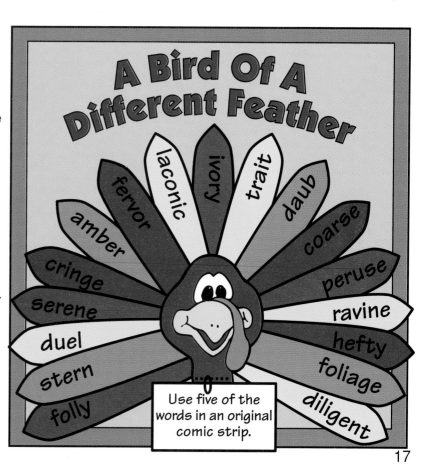

17

Create this "fan-tastic" Thanksgiving bulletin-board display sure to please! Make the turkey's body by gluing small squares of tissue paper onto a large, poster-board circle. Attach the turkey head (pattern on page 68) to the body. Have students fanfold colorful construction or tissue paper for the tail. This is a bulletin board that even old Tom Turkey would be proud of!

Vivian Campbell
Grandview School
Piscataway, NJ

Generate a bounty of gratitude with this unique display and classroom challenge. Enlarge and color the turkey pattern on page 69 to mount on the board. Duplicate the form on page 70 on yellow construction paper. Challenge your students to complete as many forms as possible in order to reach a class total of one million items for which students are thankful! If desired, invite another class or an entire grade level to join you in the fun.

Julia Alarie—Gr. 6, Essex Middle School, Essex, VT

Winter

Winter Bulletin Boards...........................

Celebrate your students' giftedness with this outstanding display. After duplicating a class set of ornament patterns on page 71, have students decorate them with markers and glitter and hang them from a bulletin-board tree. Provide each student with a cardboard rectangle to cover with holiday wrapping paper. Add a ribbon bow and a gift tag labeled with the student's name and his particular strength or "gift" (see below). Arrange the presents around the base of the tree.

William Turner—Gr. 5, Thaxton Elementary, Thaxton, VA

Make your classroom more cozy with a holiday display full of warm wishes. First have each student create a construction-paper quilt square similar to the examples shown. Then have him use paper, yarn, and bits of cloth to create a face that resembles his own. Arrange the quilt squares on a white background and add a scalloped dust ruffle across the bottom. Mount several of the faces in a row across the top. Replace the faces every few days until each student has displayed his creation.

Julia Alarie—Gr. 6, Essex Middle School, Essex, VT

Wrap up the year with a display of your students' favorite books. Give each student a white, paper rectangle to decorate as a gift box. Have the student top her "box" with the bow and tag patterns on page 72. After each student decorates her package and bow, have her label the tag with the title and author of her favorite book. Add a festive touch by mounting ribbon, wrapping-paper rolls, scissors, and tape on the bulletin board.

Catha Stroupe and Beth White—Media Center, Central Middle School, Dobson, NC

"How would you promote world peace?" Encourage students to think about this question; then have each child write his idea on a half sheet of paper. Duplicate the dove pattern (page 73) for each student. Instruct each student to cut out the pattern and place its dotted edge on the fold of a folded piece of white paper; then have him trace the pattern and cut it out. After unfolding the cutout, have the student glue it and his writing on a sheet of dark blue paper as shown. Have him label his dove cutout with one of the peace words listed on page 73.

adapted from an idea by Pamela J. Fox—Gr. 4, Bixby Public Schools, Bixby, OK

HAVING A BALL!

Share favorite holiday traditions with a cheery display! Have each student decorate an eight-inch circle with a holiday design. On the ball, have him glue an index card on which he's described a holiday tradition that his family enjoys. For each child, duplicate a copy of the ornament top on page 74 on gray construction paper. Have students glue the ornament tops to their artwork. Suspend the giant ornaments on varying lengths of ribbon on your bulletin board and a neighboring wall space.

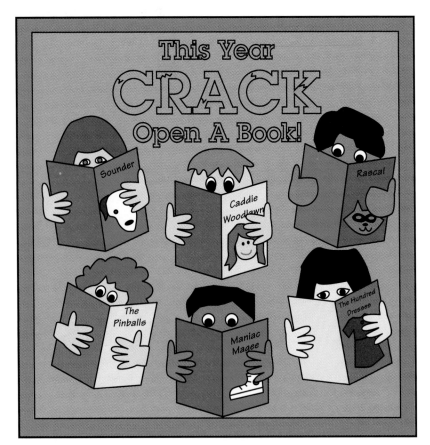

If your New Year's resolution is to encourage reading, here's the display for you! Have each student fold a 12" x 18" piece of construction paper in half and decorate it to resemble the cover of a favorite book. After completing the cover, the student makes an oaktag head and pair of hands to glue onto the book as shown. Encourage students to use 3-D touches such as curled paper for hair. Use this idea for a great Open House display as well!

Sandra McKee—Gr. 4
Woodstock Elementary
Memphis, TN

22

Ring in the new year with a colorful display that's a snap to make. Cut large balloons from construction paper for the top of your board. Add paper streamers or curling ribbon found at many card shops or party supply stores. Dot the board with colored markers to make "confetti." Help students brainstorm a list of possible resolutions for the new year; then have each child write his resolution on a copy of the pattern on page 75. Don't forget to add your own resolution to the board!

Laura Gayle McCord, Whitesburg Elementary, Carrollton, GA

Say good-bye to the old year and hello to the new with a simple display that students can make. Cover a bulletin board with white paper. Add a title and poem similar to the ones shown. Duplicate the patterns (page 76) on yellow construction paper. Have each student write his name on a horn before cutting it out and posting it on the board. To complete the display, have each child draw "music" coming from his horn in the form of a New Year's resolution. Add colorful confetti dots and brightly colored ribbons for a festive touch.

Diane McMichael—Grs. 3–5, Jefferson Elementary, Parkersburg, WV

What's a new year without some super goals? Instruct each student to brainstorm a list of New Year's resolutions. Duplicate the football and helmet patterns on pages 77 and 78. Have each student write his resolutions on a football. Display each football with a helmet that has been decorated with a student's photo and his favorite team colors. Write a list of class resolutions on a football pattern; then post it with a class picture as shown.

Michelle Calcaterra—Gr. 5, Rock Springs Elementary, Apopka, FL

Celebrate the birthday of Dr. Martin Luther King, Jr., with this dramatic bulletin board. Instruct your students to work in pairs to research facts about King's life. Have each pair summarize its research in a paragraph and add an illustration. Mount these projects on red construction paper; then arrange them on the board on top of a large black triangle. Post a portrait of King at one end of the triangle as shown.

After discussing the goals Dr. Martin Luther King, Jr., had for solving problems peacefully, have each student think of someone in his own life with whom he needs to make peace. Have the student write a peace treaty naming that person, explaining why he wants peace with him or her, and stating the terms of the peace. Instruct the student to copy his treaty onto a dove pattern (page 79); then have him trace and cut out another pattern from black paper. Staple each white dove over a black dove to create a shadow effect.

Kelly L. Simpson—Gr. 4, Newbury Elementary, Howell, NJ

Display students' writings on this winter wonderland. Staple three white circles to the board, stuffing them with tissue paper for a 3-D effect. Use twigs and other art materials to complete the snowman. Have each student tear a large circle from an 8" x 8" sheet of white tissue paper; then have her copy her winter poem or haiku onto the circle using a black felt-tip pen. Next have the student glue three 9" x 1/2" strips of brightly colored paper to make an asterisk shape and glue the poem in the center of this shape. Staple these poetic snowflakes around the snowman.

Dale Lindberg—Gr. 5, Stone Scholastic Academy, Chicago, IL

Creative interpretations of what "Winter Is" highlight this bulletin board. Have students write their winter stories on white, construction-paper penguins duplicated from the pattern on page 80. Mount student work as shown. Place student-made snowflakes randomly around the board. For a 3-D effect, pin the snowflakes so that they stand out slightly from the bulletin board.

Catherine Cannon—Gr. 4–6 Special Education, Glendale Elementary School, Glen Burnie, MD

Show off your students' valentine papers and projects on this bulletin board. Enlarge and color the artwork on the open worksheet on page 81. Have students complete assignments on duplicated copies of page 81; then have them make an assortment of valentine conversation hearts to complete the display.

Mary F. Williams—L.D. Tutor, H.V. Bear Elementary School, Miamisburg, OH

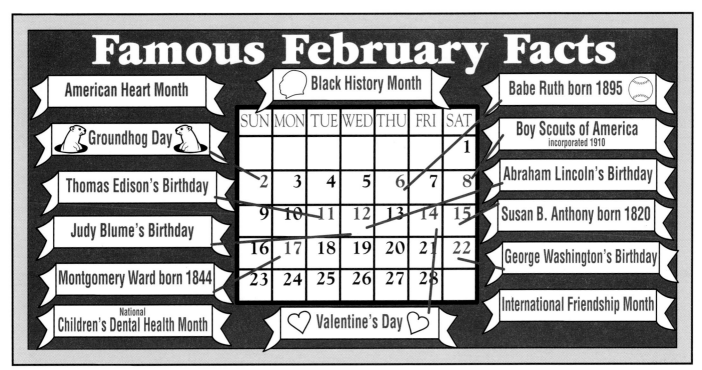

Famous February Facts

American Heart Month

Groundhog Day

Thomas Edison's Birthday

Judy Blume's Birthday

Montgomery Ward born 1844

National
Children's Dental Health Month

Black History Month

SUN	MON	TUE	WED	THU	FRI	SAT
						1
2	3	4	5	6	7	8
9	10	11	12	13	14	15
16	17	18	19	20	21	22
23	24	25	26	27	28	

Valentine's Day

Babe Ruth born 1895

Boy Scouts of America
incorporated 1910

Abraham Lincoln's Birthday

Susan B. Anthony born 1820

George Washington's Birthday

International Friendship Month

February's teeming with important events and dates! Highlight them with this easy-to-make bulletin board. Mount a poster-board calendar with special dates written in red. On sentence-strip banners, write special events and dates in February; have students illustrate each with a symbol or picture. Use red yarn to connect the banners to the appropriate days of the month. Challenge students to come up with lesser-known or unusual facts about February.

Lisa Hoffman—Gr. 4, Bryson Elementary School, Simpsonville, SC

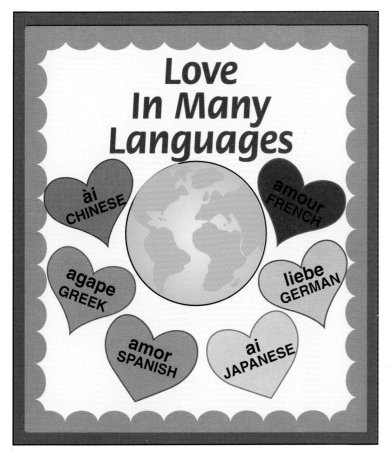

Love In Many Languages

ài CHINESE

amour FRENCH

agape GREEK

liebe GERMAN

amor SPANISH

ai JAPANESE

No matter how you spell it, it's the season for love! Mount an enlarged and colored copy of the globe pattern on page 92 on the board; then surround it with hearts labeled with the spellings of *love* in several languages. (See the heart patterns on page 82.) If desired, have students add magazine pictures of children around the world to this heartwarming display.

Mary F. Williams—L.D. Tutor
H.V. Bear Elementary School
Miamisburg, OH

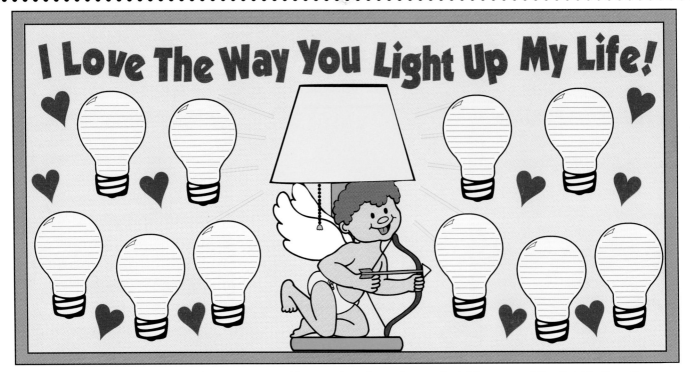

Who really lights up your life? Ask students this question; then give each child a copy of the light-bulb pattern on page 83. Have the student write about a person he or she admires and why. Enlarge and color the lamp/cupid pattern on page 84. Post it on the board with the light bulbs and student-made hearts as shown. Use yellow chalk to draw "beams" shining from the lamp.

adapted from an idea by Barbara Alport—Gr. 4, Newbury School, Howell, NJ

This valentine bulletin board encourages creative thinking. Enlarge, color, and cut out the quiver pattern on page 85. Prepare several heart shapes (see the pattern on page 82) and label each one with a "heart" phrase. Display two or three hearts on the bulletin board daily. Instruct children to write paragraphs describing what they think these phrases mean. Collect and discuss suggestions. Other possible phrases: have a heart; pulling at my heartstrings; you're a heartbreaker; getting to the heart of the matter; zing went the strings of my heart; you wear your heart on your sleeve.

Joan Joseph
Florence, KY

Spring

Spring Bulletin Boards....................................

To help students recognize each other's positive traits, give each child a class list. Students write a positive comment beside every classmate's name before turning in their sheets. Each Monday post a large silhouette of a Student of the Week; then add seasonal cutouts (such as hearts in February and shamrocks in March) labeled with the comments about the child taken from the sheets.

Peg Pilgrim—Gr. 5, Smith Avenue Elementary School, Westfield, MA

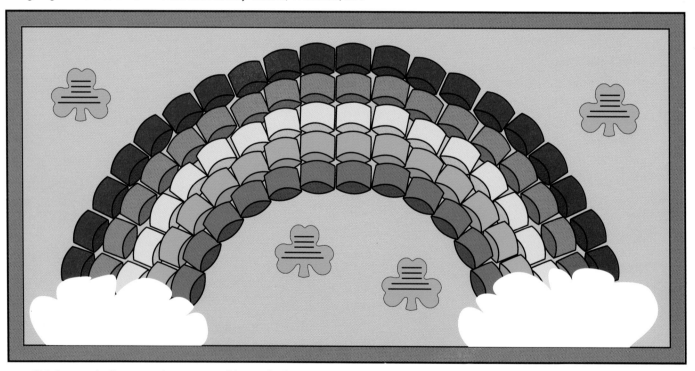

Brighten a hallway or classroom with a colorful display made entirely by students. Have children make a giant rainbow using construction-paper chains. Display original writings on cut-out shamrocks (pattern on page 87) in March and paper flowers in April.

Kathy Crocker—Gr. 4, Belton, MO

Here's a "spud-tacular" display that's just right for the mischievous month of March! Have each student cut a potato shape from his own paper; then have him glue a pair of large wiggle eyes to the cutout. To finish his spud, the child glues paper facial features, clothing, and hair to his potato.

Traci Baker—Gr. 4, Bixby, OK

Are you in luck! Here's an easy-to-make St. Patrick's Day display that doubles as a learning center. Enlarge and color the leprechaun pattern on page 86. Post it on the board with green shamrocks (pattern on page 87) labeled with seasonal learning tasks. On the stem of each shamrock, write the number of bonus points a student can earn for successfully completing the activity. Get started with the following tasks:

- Write a story about the luckiest day you've ever had.
- Read about Saint Patrick. Share your findings with the class.
- Write a short skit about St. Patrick's Day. Perform it with some friends.
- Read a library book about St. Patrick's Day. Give an oral book report.
- List as many green things as you can.
- Write a news broadcast about St. Patrick's Day.
- Design an unusual article of clothing to wear in a St. Patrick's Day parade.
- Write a fact about St. Patrick's Day in code. Give it to a friend to decode.

Kay Bindrim—Gr. 6
Parker Middle School
Rocky Mount, NC

This pot of gold brings a treasure that can be shared by all. Mount a colorful rainbow on your bulletin board. Enlarge and color the pot-of-gold pattern on page 88. Mount the pot of gold at the rainbow's end. It's always the season for kindness!

Debbie Wiggins, Myrtle Beach Elementary, Myrtle Beach, SC

Grow a garden of student-made journal starters with a bright display. Divide the class into pairs; then have each pair use the instructions on page 89 to make a giant zinnia. On a large paper leaf, have each student write a journal starter such as, "My greatest achievement is…." Mount the zinnias and leaves on a board as shown. When students need a journal idea, all they have to do is head to their garden of ideas!

adapted from an idea by Julie Johnson—Grs. 4–5, Colonial Hills School, Houston, TX

Name Drops

An April shower of "name drops" creates a striking display for creative writing. Enlarge and color the duck pattern on page 90. Each child writes his name vertically along the left edge of a raindrop cutout. Next he writes a poem about himself, starting a new line with each letter of his name. Be sure to include a raindrop poem about yourself!

Lisa L. Baker—Gr. 5, Christiansburg Elementary School, Christiansburg, VA

Build graphing skills with a student-centered bulletin board. Give each child an eight-inch square of white construction paper. On his paper, each student draws a favorite spring symbol (baseball, flower, raindrop, kite, bee, etc.). He adds his name to the drawing, colors it, then cuts it out. To make the graph, draw five or six columns on white background paper. Write the title of the graph on a sentence strip. Add index card headings, labeled with specific spring activities. Each student chooses his favorite activity and posts his drawing in the appropriate column. After discussing the graph and incorporating it in a math lesson, change the title and headings to create a new one. Or allow student volunteers to select their own titles and headings.

33

Put out the welcome mat for spring with this eye-catching bulletin board. Cut out a large paper umbrella and mount it on your bulletin board. Have students make paper flowers, butterflies, birds, and other signs of spring to insert in and around the umbrella.

Ann Higgins, St. Davids, Ontario, Canada

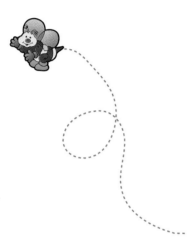

With the spread of spring fever, now's the perfect time to remind students of important study habits. Enlarge and color the rabbit pattern on page 91. Write the reminders on construction-paper clouds, outlining each cloud with a different color of marker. Have your students suggest other "hoppin' good" study habits to add to the display.

Time to trash your classroom! Observe Earth Day and heighten an awareness of our solid waste problem by creating a bulletin board of throwaways. Have each child bring in a *cleaned* piece of trash that his or her family normally throws away. Mount the trash on a bulletin board decorated with a large, painted Earth (see the pattern on page 92).

Jeff Bass—Gr. 5, Lincoln Elementary, Wauwatosa, WI

Somewhere over the rainbow is this creative-writing bulletin board! Duplicate the rainbow pattern on page 93 on white construction paper. Have each student color and cut out his rainbow. On a paper cloud, have the child write his own "reason for rainbows." Help students by posting starters such as, "I like rainbows because…," "Rainbows are…," "The colors of the rainbow remind me of…," and "At the end of the rainbow you'll find…."

Mary Williams—L.D. Tutor, H. V. Bear School, Miamisburg, OH

Take down that May bulletin board—but leave the background paper right where it is! Add the title "I'll Never Forget When…"; then place a box of colorful markers nearby. Allow each child to label the board with a special memory of the year. Encourage students to decorate the display with construction-paper confetti.

Sandy Hawkins, Richmond Elementary, Fleetwood, PA

Your students will get a real kick out of this end-of-the-year display! Duplicate student copies of the boot pattern on page 95; then enlarge, color, and cut out the cowboy pattern on page 94. Have each student label and personalize his boot with markers, glitter, sequins, and other art materials. Staple each boot to the board, leaving the top unstapled. Insert folded copies of a graduation certificate inside the cutouts to officially "boot" each student into the next grade.

adapted from an idea by Kay Vetter—Gr. 4, Central City Public School, Central City, NE

Turn the page on another year! Cut out a large book shape from bulletin-board paper and mount on the board. In the center of the book, display a summary of the year written in book-report form as shown. Finish the display by adding photos taken throughout the year and student-written captions.

Debra Little—Gr. 5, El Dorado Springs R-2 Elementary School, El Dorado Springs, MO

Have each student draw a self-portrait (from the shoulders up) on 12" x 18" white paper, being sure to use the entire sheet. After students cut out their drawings, staple them along the bottom of the board. (Mount extras on top of the board or along the sides.) Next pin a topic under the title. Have students write their opinions on the topic on cut-out speech bubbles. Use this board year-round by featuring a new topic each week!

Another chapter in your students' lives comes to an end! This BIG book is the perfect publication for recording their memories. First attach a 20" x 26" sheet of colorful paper to a small bulletin board. Then fold three 18" x 24" sheets of colorful construction paper in half. Staple the three sheets (on the crease) to the board as shown. Provide each student with an 8 1/2" x 11" sheet of white paper. On the sheet, have the student write paragraphs, poems, phrases, sentences, and/or descriptive words that tell about the past year. Encourage students to add colorful illustrations as well. Glue two completed student sheets to each side of a large page to complete this unique class book.

Let your students show how proud they are for having "licked" another school year. Enlarge, color, and cut out the monkey pattern on page 96. Provide students with 9" x 6" pieces of colorful construction paper. Have each student cut out a Popsicle® shape from her sheet. On the shape, have her write her name and a sentence describing one positive experience of the school year. After gluing each cutout to a Popsicle® stick, attach it to the board as shown. What a "delicious" way to highlight student accomplishments!

Susan Bell—Gr. 5, Lincoln Elementary, St. Charles, MO

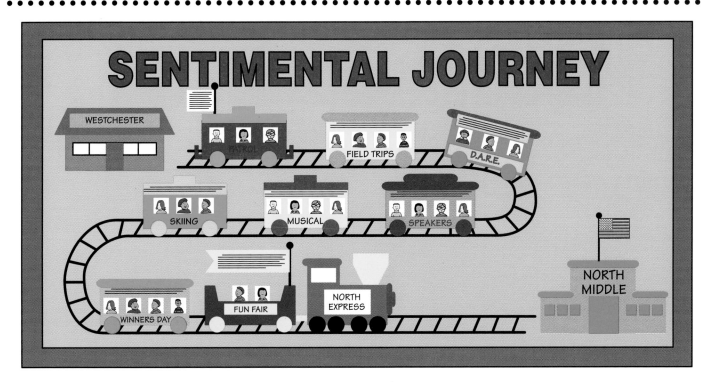

Take a sentimental, end-of-the-year journey with this colorful, student-made display. Assign each cooperative group one major event of the school year to describe in a paragraph. Instruct the groups to rewrite their final drafts on copies of the train car patterns on pages 97 and 98. Ask students to add "passengers" (their school pictures) gazing out of the car windows. Use black yarn for the railroad track. Add a photo or drawing of your school at the beginning of the track and an illustration of the students' next destination at the end. When the cars are completed, arrange them in order behind the engine.

Nancy M. Grow—Gr. 5, Westchester Elementary, Kirkwood, MO

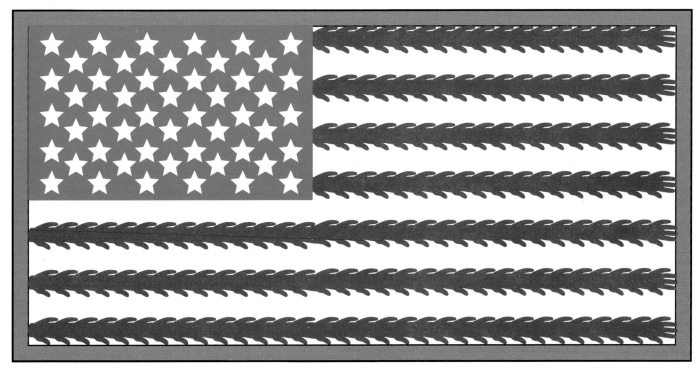

Celebrate Flag Day (June 14) with this easy-to-make board that students can work on during free time. Attach 50 white stars to a sheet of blue oaktag. Instruct students to trace their hands several times on red construction paper. Have each child cut out his or her hand patterns and attach them to the board to create the flag's stripes.

Susan White—Gr. 4, St. Timothy School, Chantilly, VA

Cross the finish line of another year with a student-made display. Mount two strips of green paper as shown. Have each student draw, color, and cut out a picture of himself running and mount on the board. For a motivational display, have students run to the finish line as they complete required assignments. Be sure to stress that it's more important to finish than to come in first!

Debra L. Cale, Niagara Falls, NY

Say thanks to your school's volunteers with a cool display. Enlarge, color, and cut out the cat pattern on page 99. Duplicate the scoop and cone patterns on page 100 on colorful construction paper. After cutting them out, label each scoop with the name of a volunteer.

Get extra mileage from this idea by using the patterns to make a back-to-school bulletin board. In August, label the scoops with the names of your new students. Post on a bulletin board with the cat character and the title, "Here's The Scoop…It's Going To Be A Cool Year!"

Wanda R. Reding
Lewis County Schools
Hohenwald, TN

Anytime

Anytime Bulletin Boards ....

Promote world peace during your studies of different wars in history with a timely display. Staple a large world map in the center of a bulletin board. (Or have students cut out and mount magazine pictures illustrating the concepts of peace.) Have each student draw and color a different country's national flag on a small index card. Post the cards around the map as a border.

Beth Gress—Gr. 6, Crosby Elementary, Harrison, OH

Salute your remarkable readers with a colorful display. In a large gumball machine (pattern on page 101) mount a colorful circle labeled with each student's name. Each time that a student completes an evaluation on a book read independently, place a star on his gumball according to the following code:

250 pages or more: 5 points = gold star
200–249 pages: 4 points = silver star
150–199 pages: 3 points = red star
100–149 pages: 2 points = green star
Less than 100 pages: 1 point = blue star
Recognize students who earn 25, 50, 75, or 100 points with special rewards or privileges.

Marilyn Davison—Grs. 5 & 6
River Oaks Elementary
Monroe, LA

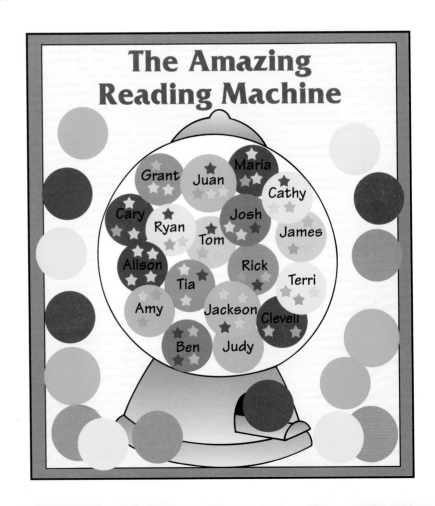

Encourage students to read a variety of books with an "m-m-m-good" motivational display. After mounting the large cone cutout (patterns on page 100) on the board and labeling its scoops with different genres of books, have each student make and label a paper cone as shown. Each time a student reads a book of a particular genre, let him staple an appropriately colored paper scoop to his cone. When a student's cone matches the large one, reward him with a certificate to an ice-cream shop.

Mary Boyle—Grs. 5-6, St. Leonard's School, Madison, NE

Recognize "toad-ally" awesome news with a board that accentuates the positive. Duplicate a supply of the toad pattern on page 102 on green construction paper. Place the patterns with a supply of scissors and fine-tipped, black markers near the display. When a student has good news to share about himself (improvement of a grade, a family trip, etc.) or a classmate ("Steve helped Gloria with her research project," etc.), let him write the news on a toad cutout and add it to the board. Encourage students to also add positive news gleaned from newspapers, magazines, and television.

adapted from an idea by Karyl Kimmel Molchan—Gr. 4, Churchill Elementary, Homewood, IL

Highlight your students' artwork year-round with this easy-to-make bulletin board. Staple a nametag for each child on the board. In September, have students draw self-portraits to display beneath their tags. Repeat the activity in June; then stuff both pictures into each child's report-card envelope. Every month from October to May, have each student display a new piece of artwork.

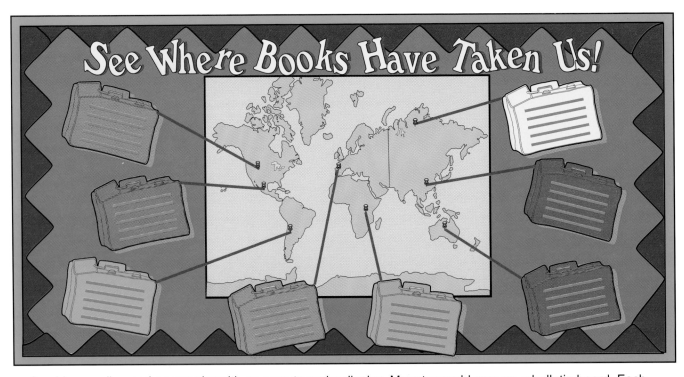

Combine reading and geography with an easy-to-make display. Mount a world map on a bulletin board. Each time your class reads a book, discuss the book's setting and locate it on the map. Label a construction-paper suitcase (pattern on page 103) with the book's title, author, and setting; then use yarn and a pushpin to connect the suitcase to the location on the map.

adapted from an idea by Marta Johnson—Gr. 4, Haw Creek School, Asheville, NC

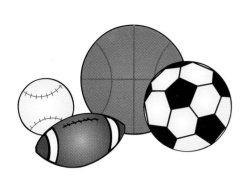

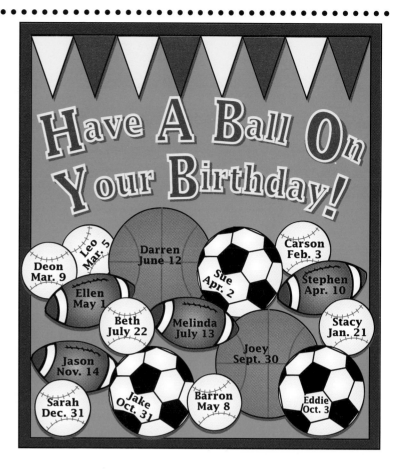

For a year-round celebration of birthdays, have students cut out all kinds of sports balls from colorful construction paper—baseballs, footballs, basketballs, etc. On each ball, write a student's name and her birthday. After laminating each ball, attach it to a bulletin board, along with the title.

Chris Murphy—Gr. 4
Emmanuel-St. Michael Lutheran School
Fort Wayne, IN

Welcome to the Writers' Block—an ideal way to show off students' writings throughout the year. Create a "block" by attaching paper houses, trees, shrubs, street signs, and lampposts to a bulletin board or wall space. Have students decorate the block to coordinate with the seasons: At Christmas, add paper wreaths, strings of paper lights, red ribbons, and cotton balls for snow; in the spring, include fresh flower beds along with kites in the sky. Mat students' writings on colorful construction paper and display them below the block. Be sure to discuss the real meaning of *writer's block* with your students.

Jean Bowen, Babb Middle School, Ellenwood, GA

Say good-bye to a hardworking student teacher with a delightful display. Have several students make a large cut-out of the student teacher to mount on the board. Give each child a 9" x 12" sheet of brown construction paper and a slightly smaller piece of black construction paper. Using white chalk, have the student write a bit of advice to the student teacher on his black paper; then have him glue it to the brown paper, rounding the corners of the finished "slate." Mount the slates on the board.

Perry Stio—Gr. 4, M. L. King School, Piscataway, NJ

Brag on your students' accomplishments with the help of the Braggin' Dragon! Enlarge and color the dragon pattern on page 104. When a child achieves a goal or does anything worth praising, write the accomplishment on a paper speech bubble, date it, and add it to the board. To make sure that everyone is recognized regularly, keep a class list handy. Place a check beside a student's name when he or she has a bubble on the board. Try to recognize each child at least once every two weeks. Send bubbles home after removing them from the board. To spread the good word about your students, post this display on your classroom door!

Traci Baker—Gr. 5
Muskogee, OK

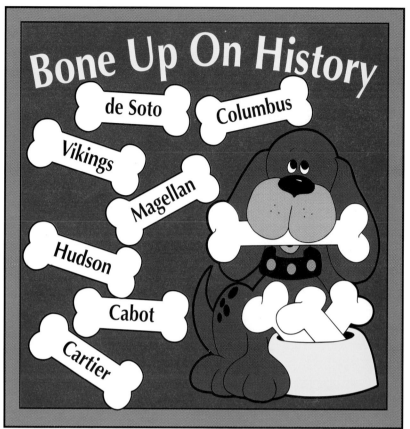

Your students can "bone up" on history facts with this fun bulletin board. Enlarge the dog pattern on page 105. Enlarge and duplicate the bone pattern also on page 105. Write history facts, important dates, famous names, etc., on the bones. Use this bulletin board to introduce a unit or as a review. Change the title and make more cut-out bones to adapt this board to other subject areas or skills.

Mary K. Good—Gr. 4
Seaford Christian Academy
Seaford, DE

Motivate reading for enjoying with a little healthy competition! Enlarge, color, and cut out the barrel-jumper pattern on page 106. Mount the pattern with a barrel-jumping challenge for your students. Each time a student reads a book, have him complete a barrel book report (page 106) to display on the bulletin board. Be sure to "roll out" a surprise celebration for a successful barrel jump!

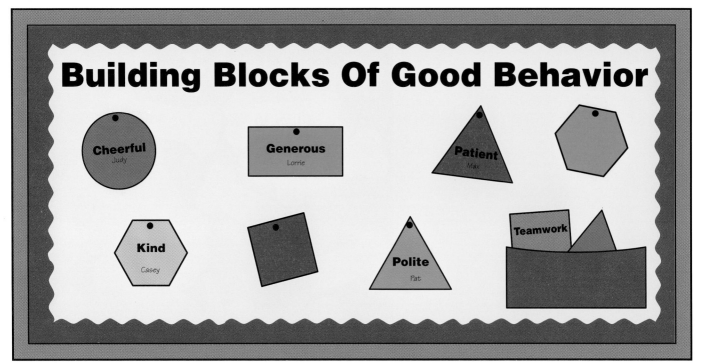

Building Blocks Of Good Behavior

This motivational behavior board will have a positive effect on your students. Make several construction-paper cutouts of each different attribute shape and label each with a positive word. Outline the shapes on the board. Each day choose one student who has demonstrated a designated behavior. Have the student sign and pin a corresponding attribute block to the board. When each shape has been filled, reward the class with a party.

Carolyn Beatty—Chapter I Grs. 4–6, Auburn Elementary School, Auburn, IL

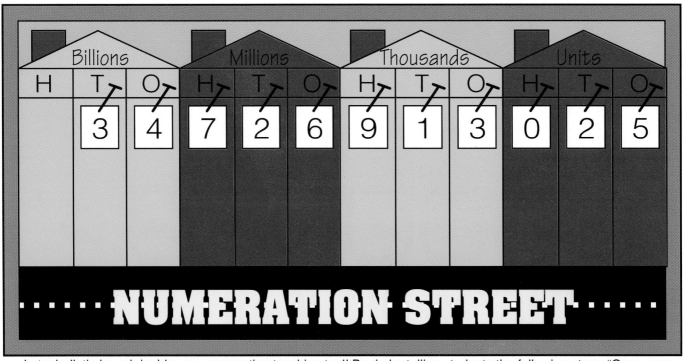

Let a bulletin board double as a numeration teaching tool! Begin by telling students the following story: "Once upon a time in Numberland there was an unusual block on Numeration Street. All of the families on this block had three children named Ones, Tens, and Hundreds. This was very confusing! The only way to identify the children was by saying their last names: Units, Thousands, Millions, and Billions." After completing the board as shown, label cut-out cards with the digits 0–9. Use the display and cards to practice place value, rounding, and other math skills.

Patsy Hill—Gr. 4, Allen Jay Elementary, High Point, NC

Launch a schoolwide drug-awareness week with a display that's out of this world! Duplicate the spaceship pattern on page 107 for each student. After writing an anti-drug message on his spaceship, each student draws a picture of himself or glues a small photo in the "driver's seat"; then he colors and cuts out the spaceship. Mount aluminum-foil stars around the ships. Invite your principal and other school personnel to add their own spaceships to the display.

Debbie Moreno—Gr. 5, Santa Fe Intermediate School, League City, TX

Watch your students race to this bulletin-board center when their work is complete. Use your last name in the title. Enlarge, color, and laminate the food patterns on page 108 and 109. Program the back of each item with an activity. When making the menu, assign an appropriate point value to each activity based on its level of difficulty. Award certificates, bonus points, or special privileges for accumulated points.

Activity Suggestions:
— List 20 different ingredients that could be included on a pizza. Now alphabetize them.
— Write the letters of the alphabet vertically. Try to think of a drink that begins with each letter (apple juice, buttermilk, cola, etc.).
— List 10 different ways to serve a hot dog.
— *Russian tea, frankfurter,* and *hamburger* each contain the name of a country or city. List 10 more foods that also contain geographical names.
— The term *french* in french fries means "to fry in deep fat until brown." List 15 other cooking terms and write their definitions.
— Research and write a paragraph to answer these two questions: How are chickens like other birds? How are they different?

Look out for this eye-catching display! Have each student post a favorite paper with a pair of specially designed glasses. Make the glasses by using the following steps:

Steps:

1. Fold a 9" x 12" piece of construction paper in half.
2. Draw and cut out the pattern as shown.
3. Cut out the centers of the glasses; then unfold the pattern.
4. Draw colorful designs on the glasses using thick lines of Elmer's GluColors®. Let the designs dry.
5. Cover the back of the glasses with regular glue; then press the glasses on top of a piece of colored plastic wrap or cellophane.
6. After the glue dries, trim the plastic wrap along the outer edges of the pattern.

Motivate students who have a hard time crossing the homework finish line! Draw a large racetrack on a bulletin board. On white construction paper, duplicate the shoe pattern on page 110 for each student. Have the student color and cut out his shoe, and label it with his name. When a student turns in all of his homework assignments on time, let him post his shoe on the track. Reward any student who keeps his shoe up all week with an inexpensive treat or a classroom privilege.

Sarah Steinwand—Gr. 5
Hayward Elementary
Sioux Falls, SD

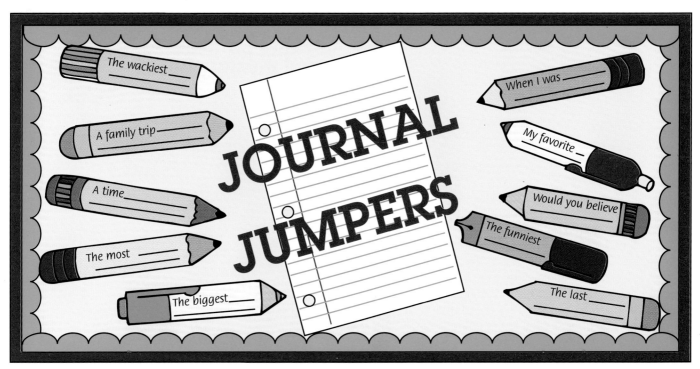

Students sometimes need a "jump start" to come up with ideas for writing in their journals. Instruct your class to turn their favorite ideas into journal starters to share with one another. Provide each student with a sentence strip. Have her decorate it so that it becomes a giant pen or pencil; then instruct her to write her topic on the strip. When a student is stumped for a writing topic, all she has to do is select one from the board.

Eileen J. Harford—Grs. 5–6, Orchard Middle School, Solon, OH

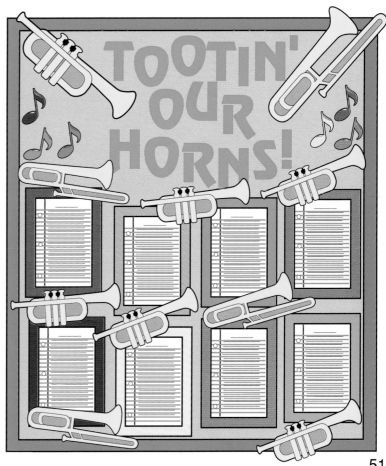

Display students' work with this colorful, eye-catching bulletin board. Duplicate four or five copies of the two horn patterns (page 76) on yellow construction paper. Mount students' papers on colorful 9" x 12" sheets of construction paper. Post the students' work, along with the horns, as shown.

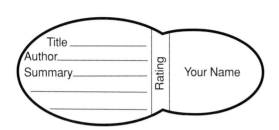

It's no mystery why intermediate kids love mystery books! Motivate an even greater interest by enlarging the detective character on page 89 and mounting it with a speech bubble as shown. Each time a student reads a mystery book, have him trace his shoe; then have him cut out the tracing. Have the student label his cutout as shown in the diagram above. Add these unusual book reports to the board for a display that's packed with suspense!

Julia Alarie—Gr. 6
Essex Middle School
Essex, VT

For an "egg-ceptionally" fun project, have each student research a famous person. After writing brief reports to share with the class, have students use a variety of art materials to decorate large egg-shaped cutouts to illustrate their famous people. In addition, have each child design a business card for his person on a small index card. Staple the business cards along the border of the board; then challenge students to match each card with its egg cutout.

Put students hot on the trail of trivia! Cut out pictures from magazines, old books, or newspapers. Mount each picture on a piece of construction paper, adding a question. Encourage students to track down answers during free time. On the day of the deadline, let students share their answers.

Tammy Jo Forgue—Grs. 5–6
Madison Junior High
Madison, ME

Let your students supply the motivation at this motivational bulletin board. Mount an enlarged version of the trophy pattern on page 111. Add the title banner and a border of red, white, and blue twisted crepe paper. Place laminated star cutouts (patterns on page 112) and a wipe-off marker in a Ziploc® bag attached to the trophy. Students label and post stars bearing personal accomplishments. Encourage students to frequently reprogram stars with their most recent accomplishments!

Debra Cale—Gr. 4, St. Stanislaus Kostka, Niagara Falls, NY

Pattern

Use with "Let's Begin The Year..." on page 6.

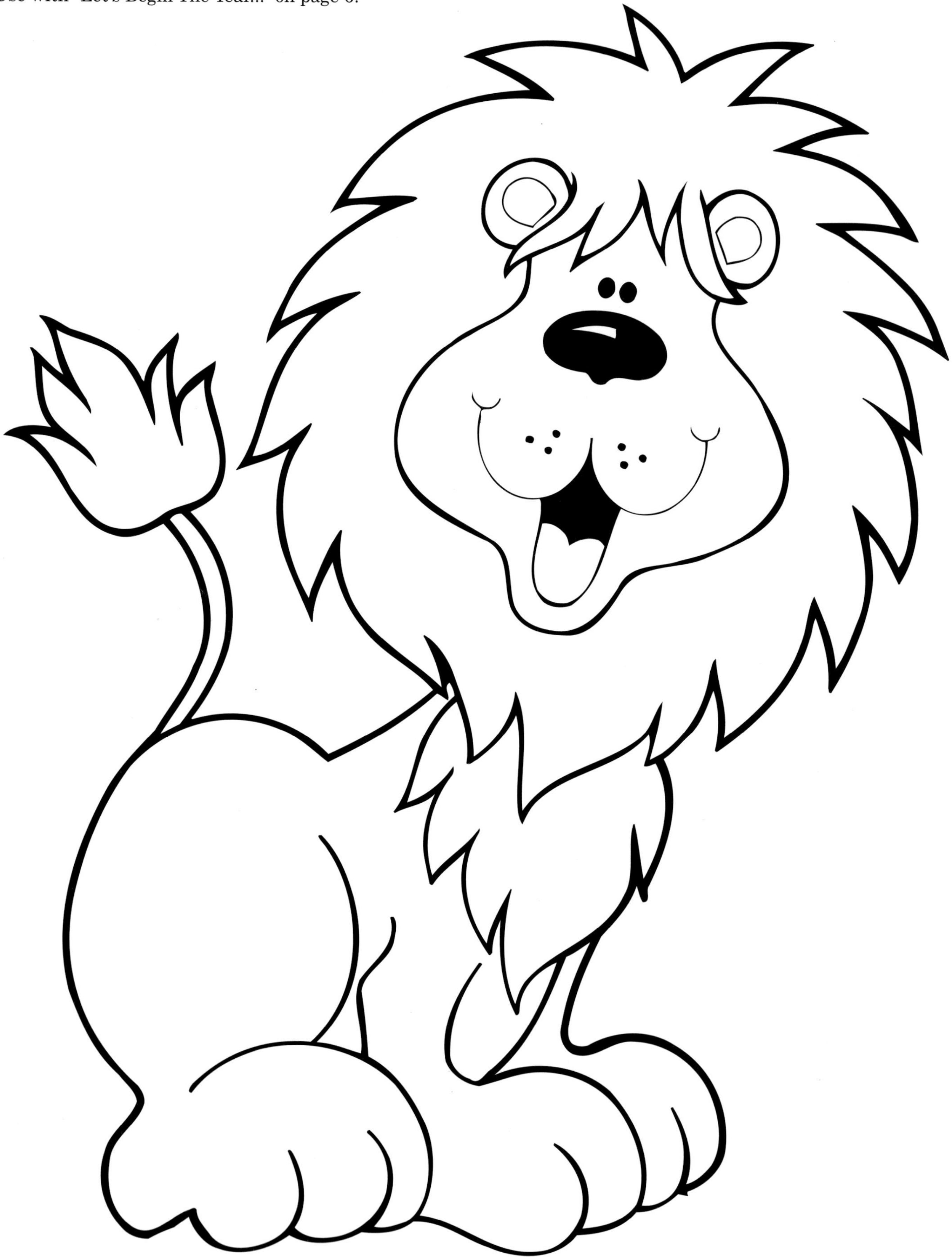

Pattern

Use with "Bite Into A Good Book!" on page 10.

Pattern

Use with "Our Compliment Tree" on page 11.

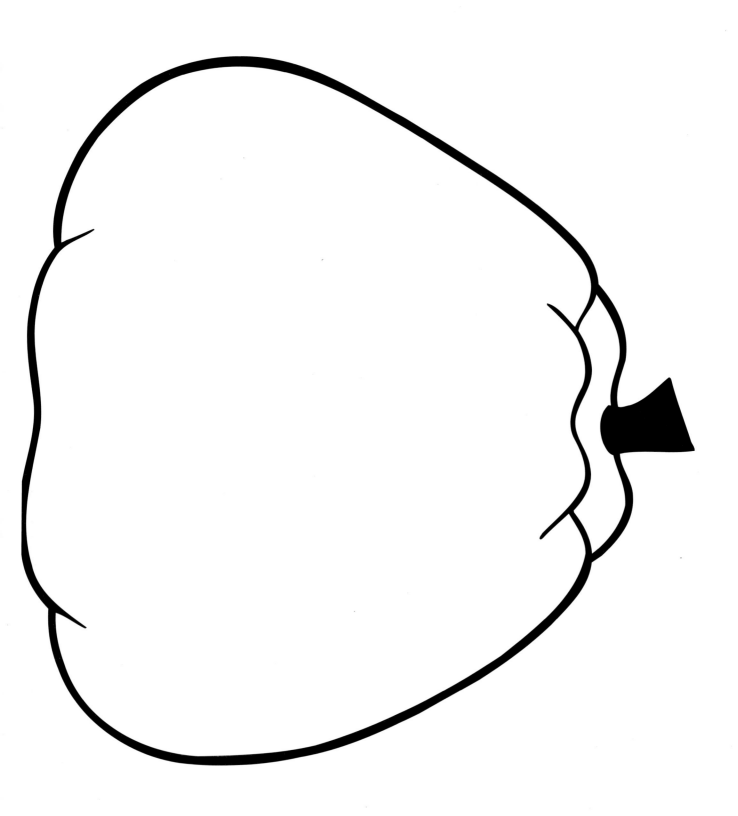

Use with "Ghoulish Graveyard" on page 13 and "Synonym Cemetery" on page 15.

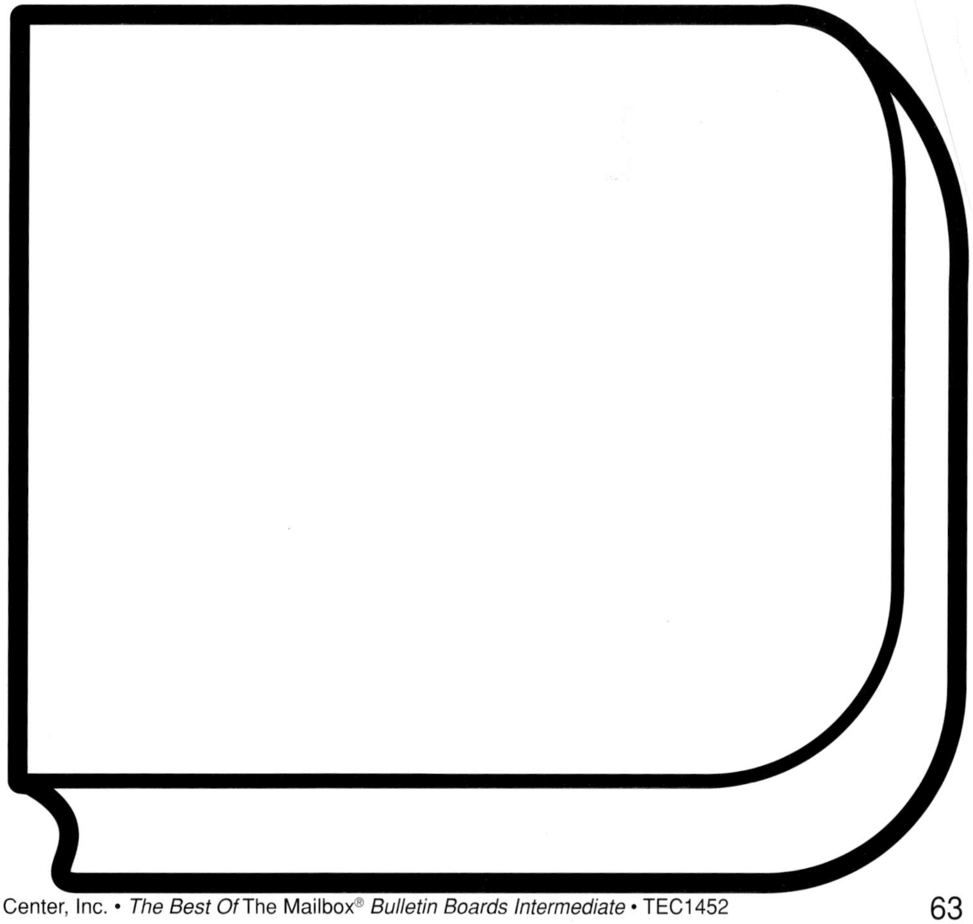

Patterns

Use with " 'Fall' Into Good Habits" on page 13, "Featuring Fall's Finest!" on page 14, and "Look Whooo's Worked Hard!" on page 17.

Pattern
Use with "An 'A+' Thanksgiving" on page 16.

Pattern

Use with "A Bird Of A Different Feather" on page 17 and "Turkey Fans" on page 18.

THANKS A MILLION!

I am thankful for my

_____
number

_____!
items

Illustrate what you're thankful for below.

Name _____

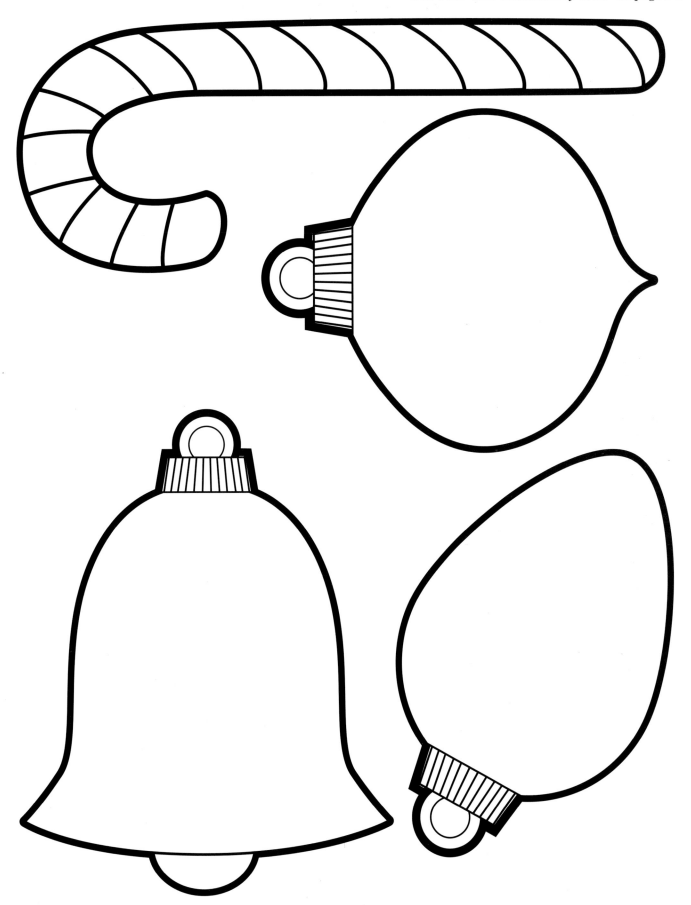

Patterns

Use with "Get All Wrapped Up In A Good Book!" on page 21.

Title: _____

Author: _____

Peace Term	Language
paix	French
paz	Spanish, Portuguese
pace	Italian
Frieden	German
vrede	Dutch
fred	Swedish, Danish, Norwegian
pokój	Polish
mír	Czechoslovakian
béke	Hungarian
ruaha	Finnish
sulh	Turkish
perdamaian	Indonesian
mir	Russian, Serbo-Croatian
ir'ni	Greek
salam	Arabic
schalom	Hebrew
scholim	Yiddish
heiwa	Japanese
amani	Swahili

Pattern

Use with "Having A Ball!" on page 22.

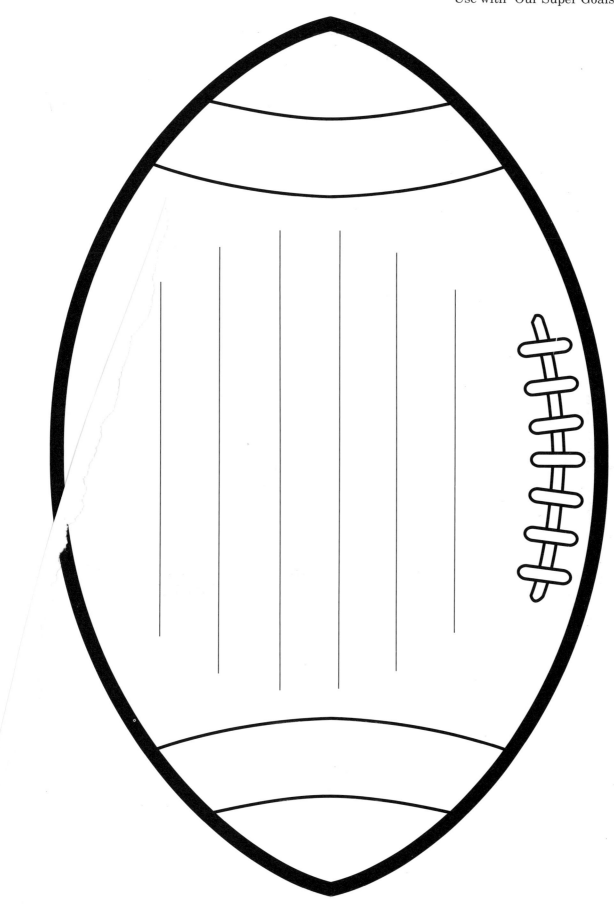

Pattern

Use with "Our Super Goals" on page 24.

Patterns

Use with "All That Jazz!" on page 23 and "Tootin' Our Horns!" on page 51.

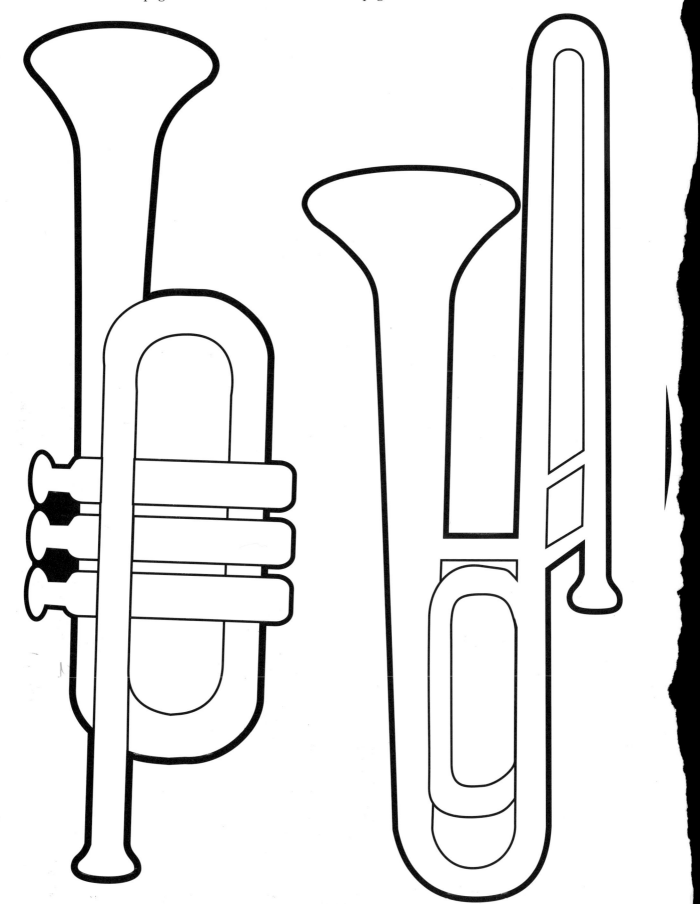

My
New Year's
Resolution

_____

date   signature

Pattern
Use with "Winter Is..." on page 26.

Name _____ *Open*

Have A Heart

When you finish, write the names of three people you admire in the heart. On the back of this sheet, list the characteristic you admire most in each person.

Note To Teacher: Program this sheet with math problems, review questions, vocabulary exercises, words to abbreviate, sentences to punctuate, or any other skill. Add lines and use for a class newsletter, a note home to parents, or handwriting practice.

Pattern

Use with "Love In Many Languages" on page 27 and "Straight From The Heart!" on page 28.

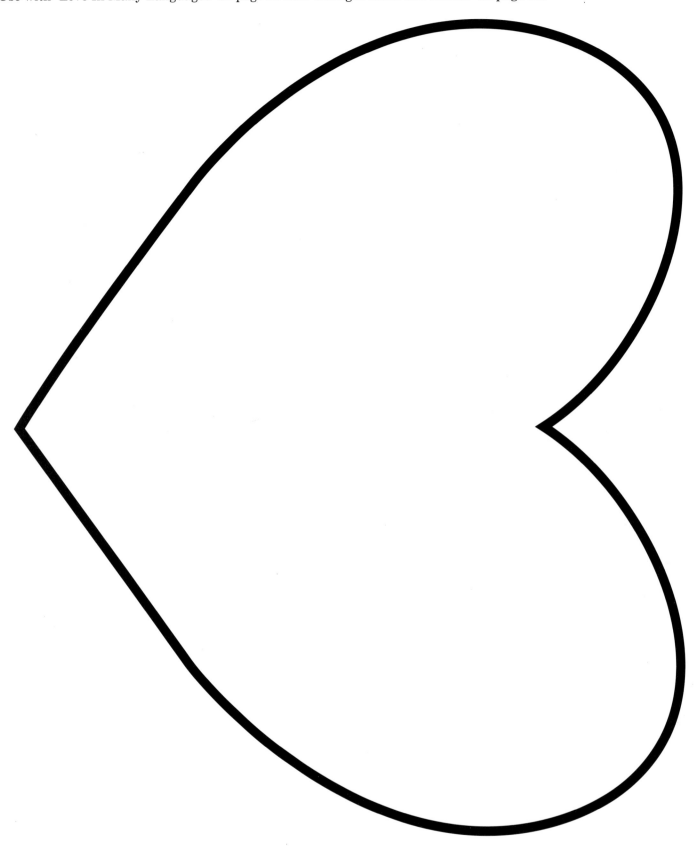

Pattern

Use with "I Love The Way You Light Up My Life!" on page 28.

Pattern

Use with the chain rainbow on page 30 and "This Could Be Your Lucky Day!" on page 31.

Pattern

Use with "Do Unto Others..." on page 32.

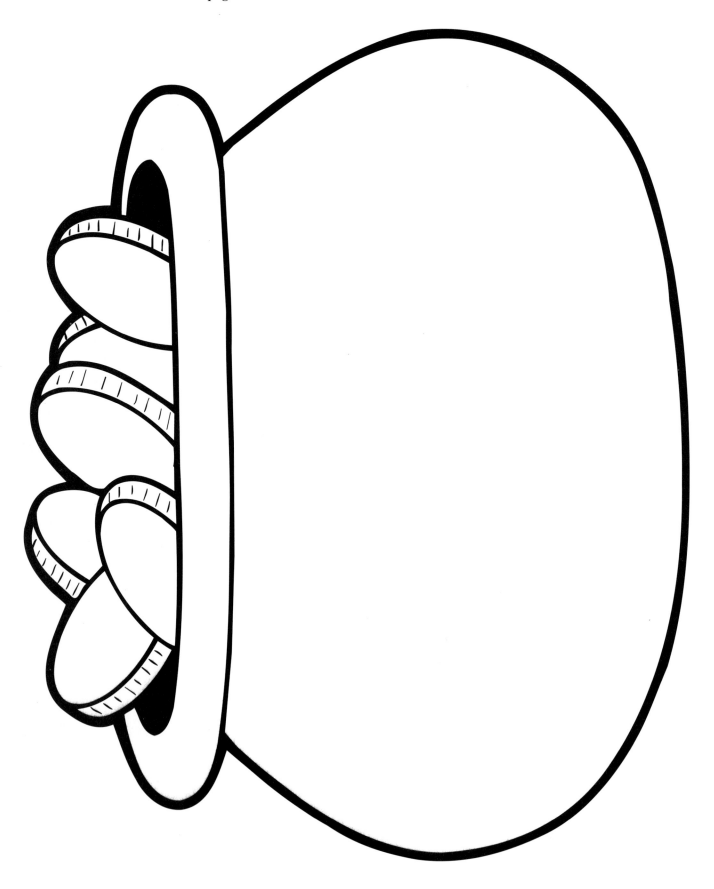

©1996 The Education Center, Inc. • *The Best Of* The Mailbox® *Bulletin Boards Intermediate* • TEC1452

Patterns

Use with "Looking For Clues To A Good Mystery Book?" on page 52.

Use with "A Garden Of Great Ideas" on page 32.

Instructions for making a zinnia:

1. Trace or draw a series of circles of varying sizes on colored ditto paper.
2. Draw a small circle (smaller than the smallest circle drawn in step 1) on a different color of paper.
3. In each circle, use a pencil to lightly draw petals as shown in the diagram.
4. Cut out all of the flowers.
5. Curl each petal of a flower around a pencil.
6. Glue the flowers together in order, with the largest flower on the bottom and the smallest, different-colored flower on top.

Pattern
Use with "Name Drops" on page 33.

Pattern

Use with "World's Best Class!" on page 7, "Love In Many Languages" on page 27, and "What On Earth Are We Doing?" on page 35.

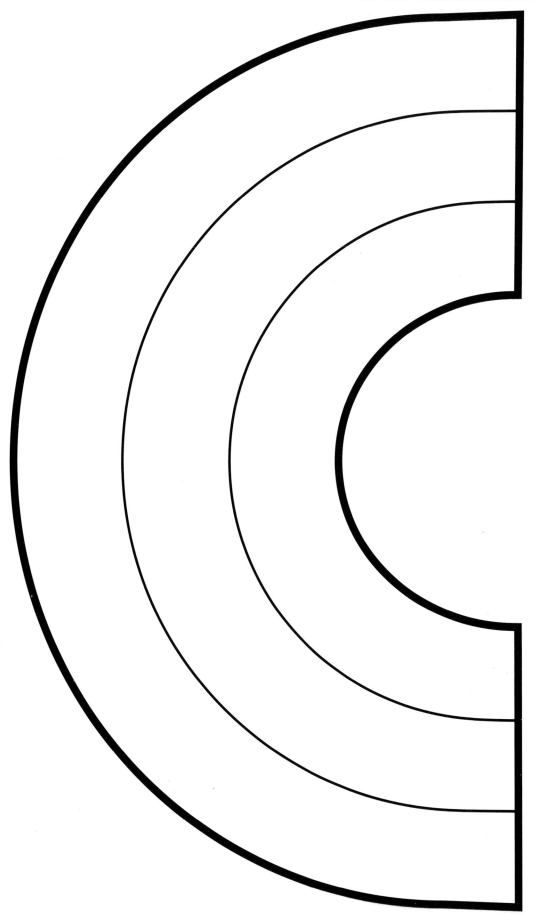

Pattern

Use with "Look Who's Being 'Booted' Out Of Fifth Grade!" on page 36.

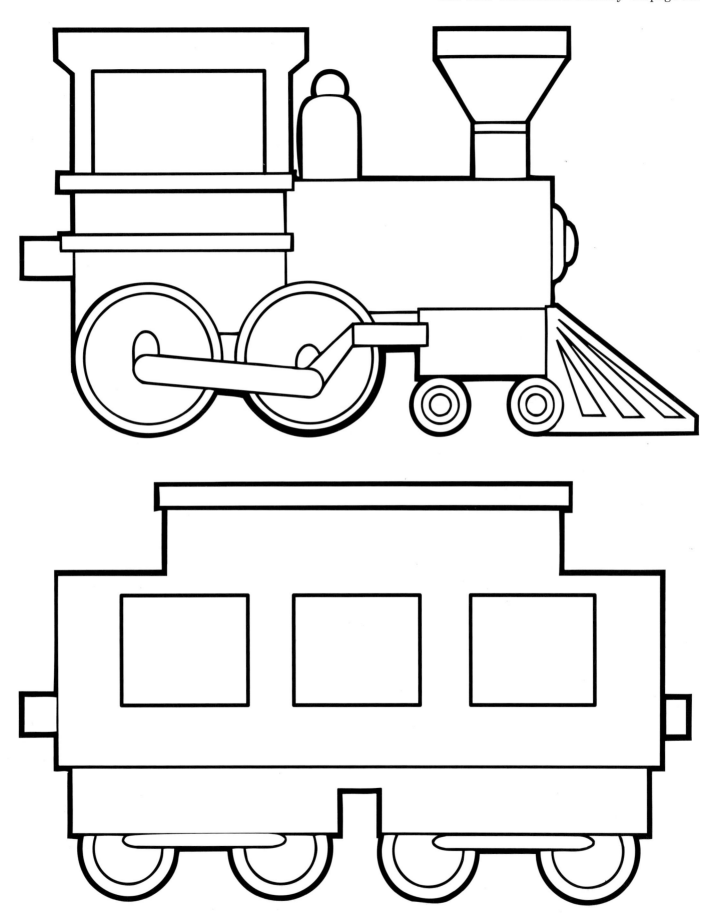

Patterns

Use with "Sentimental Journey" on page 39.

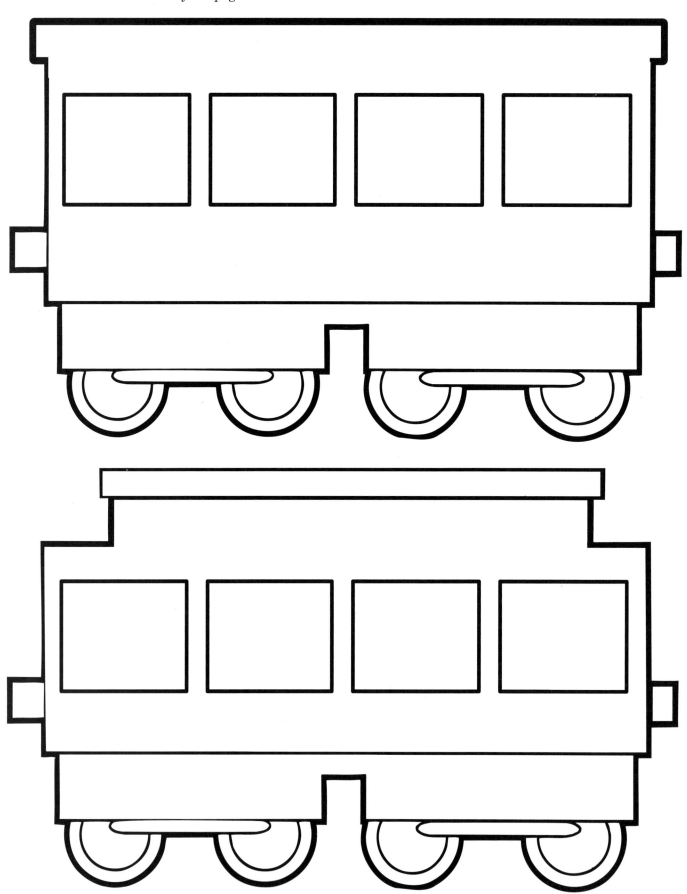

Patterns

Use with "Here's The Scoop...Our Volunteers Are Great!" on page 40 and "For A Cool Treat...Books Can't Be Beat!" on page 43.

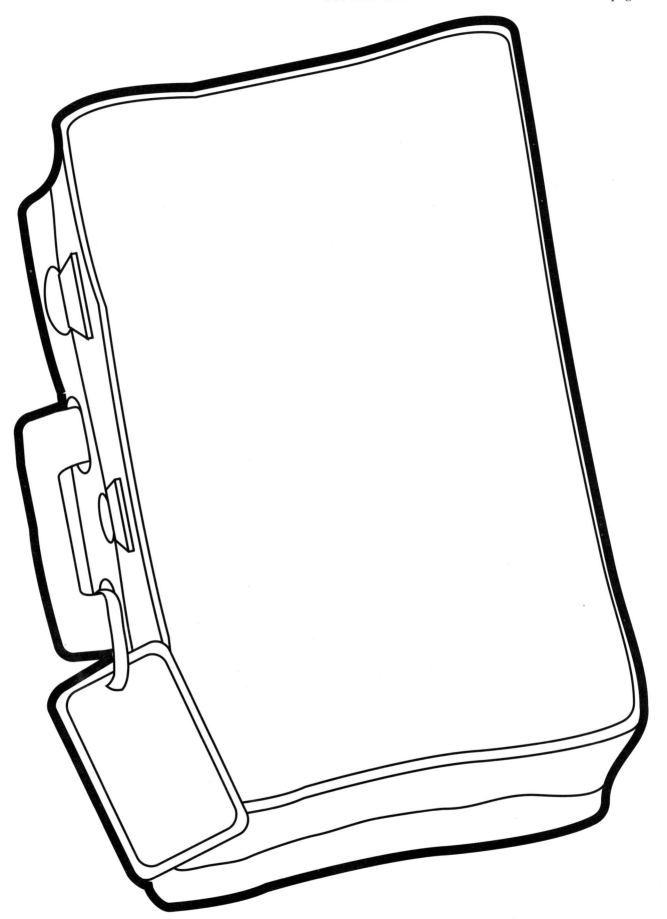

Use with "Tickle Your Funny Bone!" on page 14 and "Bone Up On History" on page 47.

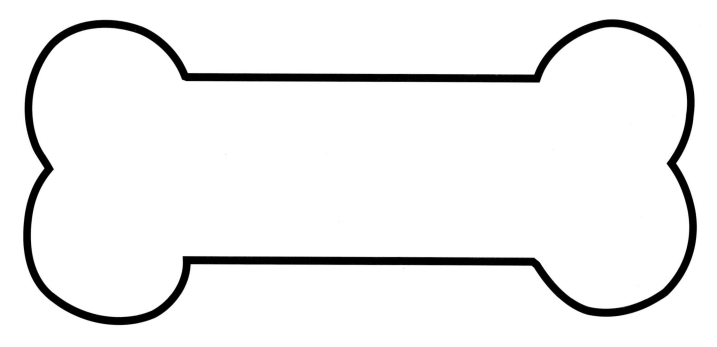

Patterns

Use with "Roll Out The Barrels!" on page 47.

Name: _____

Title: _____

Author: _____

The setting: _____

The main character: _____

The best part: _____

Use with "Let's Have A Drug-Free Galaxy!" on page 49.

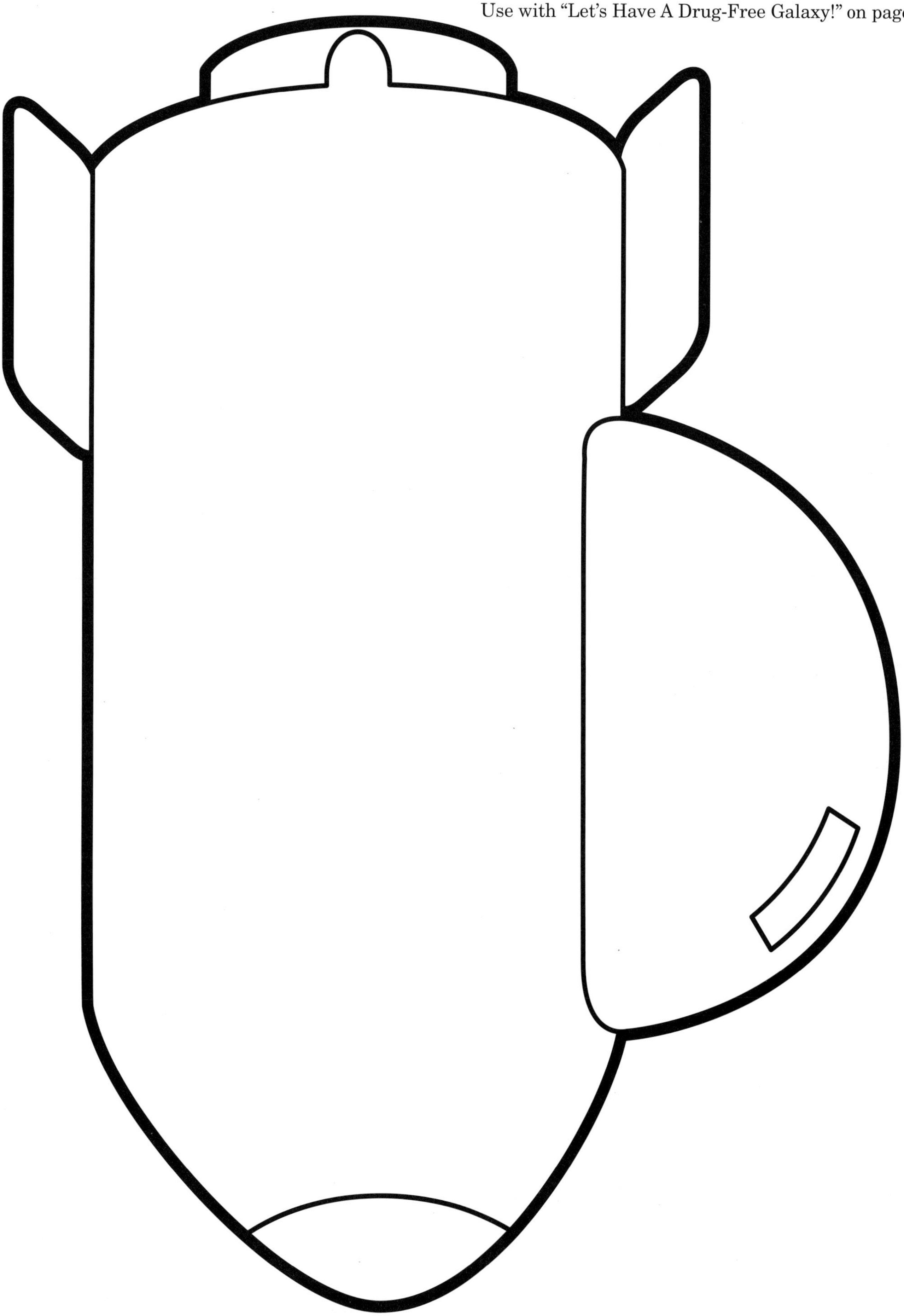

Patterns

Use with "Badden's Takeout" on page 49.

©1996 The Education Center, Inc. • *The Best Of* The Mailbox® *Bulletin Boards Intermediate* • TEC1452

Pattern

Use with "Stay On Track!" on page 50.

Patterns
Use with "Star Students" on page 53.

Pattern

Use with "Homework: Don't Leave Home Without It!" on page 12.

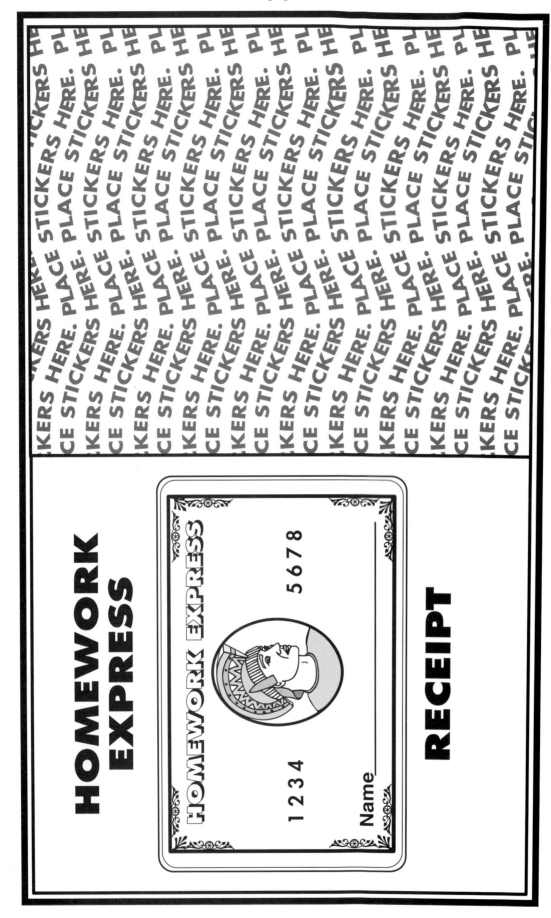

PLACE STICKERS HERE.

HOMEWORK EXPRESS

HOMEWORK EXPRESS

1234   5678

Name_____

RECEIPT

Patterns

Use with "We're In The Helping 'Mooood'!" on page 7.